10 9 8 7 6 5 4 3 2 1

Produced by Hollan Publishing, Inc.
100 Cummings Center, Suite 125G
Beverly, MA 01915
© 2008 by Hollan Publishing, Inc.

Published by Sterling Publishing Co., Inc.
387 Park Avenue South, New York, NY 10016

Distributed in Canada by Sterling Publishing
c/o Canadian Manda Group, 165 Dufferin Street
Toronto, Ontario, Canada M6K 3H6
Distributed in the United Kingdom by GMC Distribution Services
Castle Place, 166 High Street, Lewes, East Sussex, England BN7 1XU
Distributed in Australia by Capricorn Link (Australia) Pty. Ltd.
P.O. Box 704, Windsor, NSW 2756, Australia

Sterling ISBN-13: 978-1-4027-5353-4
         ISBN-10: 1-4027-5353-5

For information about custom editions, special sales, premium and corporate purchases, please contact Sterling Special Sales Department at 800-805-5489 or specialsales@sterlingpublishing.com.

Feline photography by Allan Penn

Cover design by Seth Dolinsky
Digital image composites by Al Mallette/Lightstream

CATAPULT

WHEN CATS FLY

Mr. Higgs

STERLING/HOLLAN
An imprint of Sterling Publishing Co., Inc.

New York / London
www.sterlingpublishing.com

Sparky

"I bet **Garfield** doesn't do his own **stunts**."

Sparky couldn't help but keep **testing** the limit of that old cliché about cats always **landing on their feet.**

Sneakers

Sneakers thought the **view** was great, but otherwise he felt the **"final frontier"** was pretty boring.

While searching for the **pet door**, Sneakers inadvertently discovered the **Gateway** to the West.

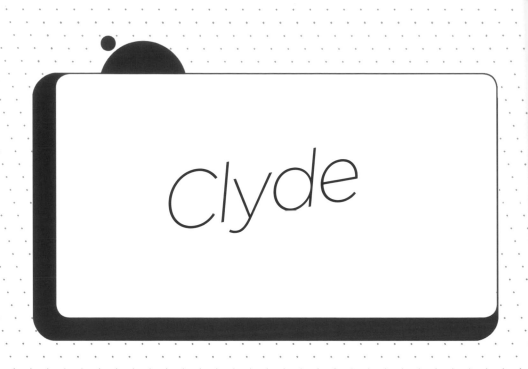

Clyde

Who puts a **kitty door** on a **spaceship** anyway?

Griffin

Griffin's new **haircut** bought him the extra **two-hundredths** of a second he needed.

Charlotte was undeniably **fond** of her new friend, but she knew that unless she grew fins or he grew feet, the relationship **wouldn't last.**

Charlotte couldn't deny that **flying south** for the winter was for the birds, but she kept reminding herself that at the end of the journey lay suntans, **mai-tais**, and **Thursday night bingo.**

Caleb

Parachute forgotten, Caleb found himself **praying**—not necessarily for a full nine lives, but for **just one more.**

Sneaking along on the family **whitewater rafting** trip seemed like a good idea at the time.

Owen

The **good news** is he would land on his feet. The **bad news** is he would land on his feet.

This time, the **tortoise** wasn't taking any chances.

Fritz

No **cats** were harmed during the **making** of this book.

But we didn't say anything about **goldfish.**

Cleo

"**Meow** meow meow meow,
Meow meow meow meow,
Meow meow meow meow meow
meow meow meow."

"**Mao** mao mao mao,
Mao mao mao mao,
Mao mao mao mao mao
mao mao mao."

Lucy

"**Mom**, Lucy is **still** following us."

The **president** would live to regret his refusal to meet with the new **PETA lobbyist.**

Mitzi

Despite being told that the show doesn't employ **actual** cats, Mitzi still allowed herself to **dream.**

Note to self:
never hide in
the parachute bag.

Tiger

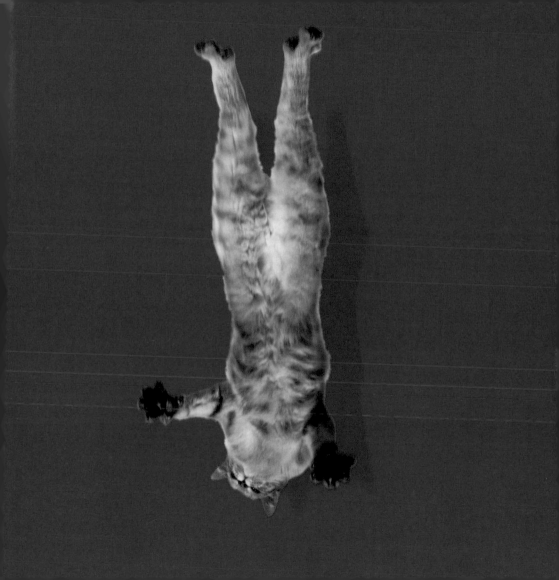

Disgruntled and **disappointed**, Tiger immediately quit his job at the **ASPCA**.

Nobody was more surprised than Tiger to discover that, at the **end** of his ninth life, he had **wings** instead of a pitchfork.